Explore
Earth's seven continents

Bobbie Kalman

Crabtree Publishing Company

www.crabtreebooks.com

Explore the Continents

A Bobbie Kalman Book

For my Aunt Margaret
You taught us how to laugh and love—and we sure do love you!

**Author and
Editor-in-Chief**
Bobbie Kalman

Editor
Kathy Middleton

Fact editor
Marcella Haanstra

Proofreader
Crystal Sikkens

Photo research
Bobbie Kalman

Design
Bobbie Kalman
Katherine Berti

**Print and production
coordinator**
Katherine Berti

Prepress technician
Katherine Berti

Illustrations
Barbara Bedell: pages 4 (frog), 8 (flower, panda bear, orangutan, and komodo
    dragon), 12 (bird, squirrel, rabbit, grasshopper, and mink), 20 (armadillo,
    beaver, and cardinal), 23 (green fish), 24 (vines, trees, birds, except parrot,
    peppers), 28 (ostrich and cuscus), 29 (coral reef), 30 (whales)
Katherine Berti: pages 4 (map), 8 (leopard and map), 12 (acorns, fish, and
    map), 17 (all except giraffe), 20 (crane, cacti, deer, snake, and map), 21 (map),
    22 (map), 23 (yellow & black fish), 24 (pudu and map), 29 (seahorse),
    30 (bird)
Robert MacGregor: pages 6, 10 (globe), 20 (globe), 28 (map), 29 (map)
Cori Marvin: page 29 (red & white fish)
Jeannette McNaughton-Julich: page 4 (dolphins)
Vanessa Parson-Robbs: pages 30 (fish), 31 (adult penguin)
Bonna Rouse: pages 12 (tree and flowers), 23 (sea turtle), 24 (parrot),
    28 (plant, mouse, and dingo), 31 (seal)
Margaret Amy Salter: pages 4 (fish), 8 (bears), 20 (loon and flowers),
    23 (yellow fish and red fish), 24 (butterflies), 29 (yellow fish),
    31 (baby penguin)

Photographs
Digital Stock: page 9 (bottom)
Digital Vision: page 19 (top)
Dreamstime: page 21 (top)
Cover and other images by Shutterstock

Library and Archives Canada Cataloguing in Publication

Kalman, Bobbie, 1947-
    Explore earth's seven continents / Bobbie Kalman.

(Explore the continents)
Includes index.
Issued also in an electronic format.
ISBN 978-0-7787-3078-1 (bound).--ISBN 978-0-7787-3092-7 (pbk.)

    1. Continents--Juvenile literature. I. Title. II. Series: Explore
the continents

G133.K343 2011   j910.914'1   C2010-904544-0

Library of Congress Cataloging-in-Publication Data

Kalman, Bobbie.
    Explore earth's seven continents / Bobbie Kalman.
        p. cm. -- (Explore the continents)
    Includes index.
    ISBN 978-0-7787-3092-7 (pbk. : alk. paper) --
    ISBN 978-0-7787-3078-1 (reinforced library binding : alk. paper)
    -- ISBN 978-1-4271-9483-1 (electronic (pdf))
    1. Continents--Juvenile literature. I. Title. II. Series.

G133.K253 2010
910.914'1--dc22

                                                    2010027349

Crabtree Publishing Company

Printed in the U.S.A./082010/BA20100709

www.crabtreebooks.com   1-800-387-7650

**Published in Canada
Crabtree Publishing**
616 Welland Ave.
St. Catharines, Ontario
L2M 5V6

**Published in the United States
Crabtree Publishing**
PMB 59051
350 Fifth Avenue, 59th Floor
New York, New York 10118

**Published in the United Kingdom
Crabtree Publishing**
Maritime House
Basin Road North, Hove
BN41 1WR

**Published in Australia
Crabtree Publishing**
386 Mt. Alexander Rd.
Ascot Vale (Melbourne)
VIC 3032

Contents

Big land areas, huge oceans

There are seven large areas of land on Earth, called **continents**. From largest to smallest, the seven continents are Asia, Africa, North America, South America, Antarctica, Europe, and Australia/Oceania. Find them on this map.

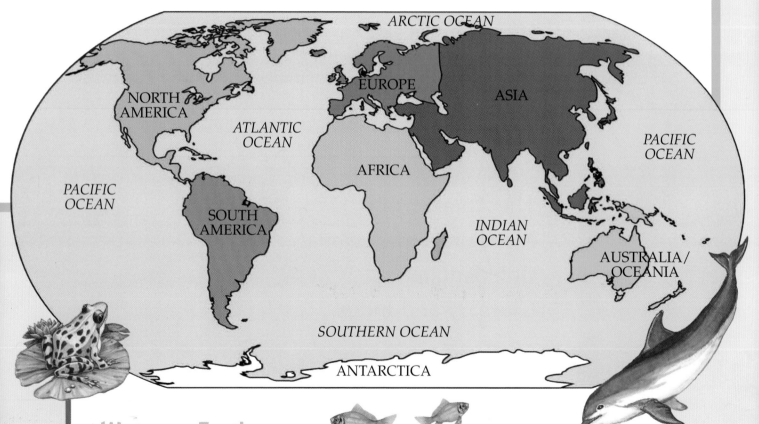

Water on Earth

Water covers about three-quarters of Earth. The blue areas on the map above show where water is on Earth. The huge areas of water are called **oceans**. Oceans contain salt water.

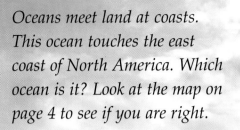

Oceans meet land at coasts. This ocean touches the east coast of North America. Which ocean is it? Look at the map on page 4 to see if you are right.

Oceans around continents

Five oceans flow around the seven continents. From largest to smallest, the oceans are the Pacific Ocean, the Atlantic Ocean, the Indian Ocean, the Southern Ocean, and the Arctic Ocean.

Looking at Earth

North, south, east, and west are the four main **directions** on Earth. The **North Pole** is the most northern point on Earth. The most southern point on Earth is the **South Pole**. The weather is cold year round near the North Pole and the South Pole.

NORTH POLE

NORTHERN HEMISPHERE

EQUATOR

SOUTHERN HEMISPHERE

SOUTH POLE

Harbor seals live in the northern waters of the Atlantic and Pacific oceans. In winter, these seals spend most of their time in the ocean. They **haul out**, or pull themselves out of water, to rest or to have their babies.

The equator

The **equator** is an imaginary line that divides Earth into two equal parts. The weather is hot year round in places near the equator.

North of the equator

The **Northern Hemisphere** is the part of Earth that is north of the equator. It is between the equator and the North Pole.

South of the equator

The **Southern Hemisphere** is the part of Earth that is south of the equator. It is between the equator and the South Pole.

Huge Asia!

There are 50 **countries** in Asia. A country is part of a continent. A country has **borders**. Borders are the areas where one country ends and another country begins. A country is run by a group of people called the **government**.

Six regions

Asia is the biggest continent! It is so big that some people group its countries together into six regions.

NORTHERN ASIA

WESTERN ASIA

CENTRAL ASIA

EASTERN ASIA

SOUTHERN ASIA

SOUTHEASTERN ASIA

1. BAHRAIN
2. KUWAIT
3. JORDAN
4. ISRAEL
5. EGYPT
6. SYRIA
7. LEBANON
8. CYPRUS
9. GEORGIA

10. ARMENIA
11. AZERBAIJAN
12. TURKMENISTAN
13. UZBEKISTAN
14. QATAR
15. OMAN
16. UNITED ARAB EMIRATES
17. AFGHANISTAN
18. PAKISTAN
19. TAJIKISTAN
20. KYRGYZSTAN

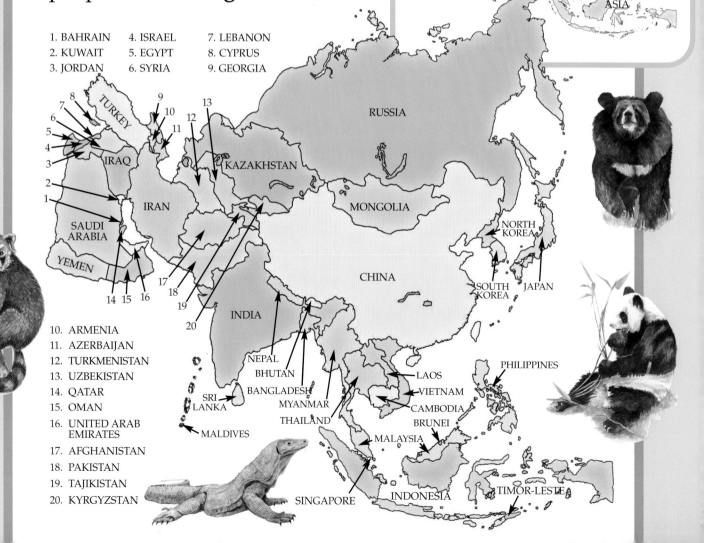

TURKEY

IRAQ

IRAN

SAUDI ARABIA

YEMEN

KAZAKHSTAN

RUSSIA

MONGOLIA

CHINA

NORTH KOREA

SOUTH KOREA

JAPAN

INDIA

NEPAL

BHUTAN

BANGLADESH

SRI LANKA

MALDIVES

MYANMAR

THAILAND

LAOS

VIETNAM

CAMBODIA

BRUNEI

PHILIPPINES

MALAYSIA

SINGAPORE

INDONESIA

TIMOR-LESTE

8

This picture shows Lake Baikal in Siberia, Russia. Lake Baikal is Earth's oldest lake with the most fresh water. Russia is the biggest country on Earth. Part of it is in northern Asia, and part is in the continent of Europe.

China is in East Asia. It has more people than any other country! The Great Wall of China is the most popular place to visit in China. This huge stone wall, built long ago, is one of Earth's largest human-made structures.

Land and sea in Asia

Three oceans touch Asia. The Arctic Ocean is along its northern coasts. The Pacific Ocean is along its eastern coasts. The Indian Ocean is along the southern coasts of Asia. There are also many **seas** along Asia's coasts. A sea is a small area of ocean with land around it. Many of the countries in Southeastern Asia and Eastern Asia are made up of thousands of **islands**. An island is land that has water all around it.

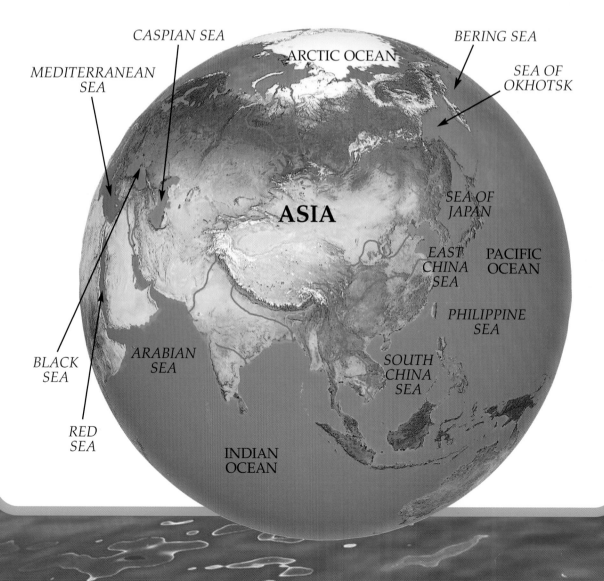

CASPIAN SEA

BERING SEA

MEDITERRANEAN SEA

ARCTIC OCEAN

SEA OF OKHOTSK

SEA OF JAPAN

ASIA

EAST CHINA SEA

PACIFIC OCEAN

PHILIPPINE SEA

BLACK SEA

ARABIAN SEA

SOUTH CHINA SEA

RED SEA

INDIAN OCEAN

Japan

The country of Japan is in Eastern Asia. It is made up of about 6,852 islands. This **archipelago**, or group of islands, is in the Pacific Ocean. Honshu is Japan's biggest island. Tokyo, Japan's capital city, is on Honshu.

India is a country in Southern Asia. It has many wonderful sights. The Taj Mahal is the most popular. It is a work of art that was built as a tomb for the wife of an emperor in the 1600s.

Petra is a very old city in Jordan, a country in Western Asia. Petra was carved out of a mountainside. The building above is part of the Monastery, which was once a temple.

Exploring Europe

Europe is joined to the continent of Asia. There are 50 countries in Europe, but several belong to both Europe and Asia. Part of Russia and Turkey, for example, are in Europe, and part are in Asia.

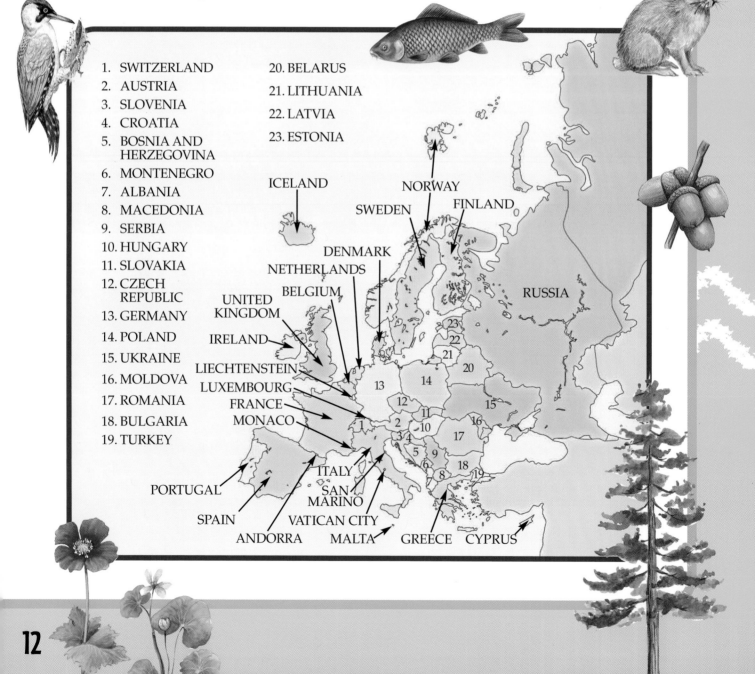

1. SWITZERLAND
2. AUSTRIA
3. SLOVENIA
4. CROATIA
5. BOSNIA AND HERZEGOVINA
6. MONTENEGRO
7. ALBANIA
8. MACEDONIA
9. SERBIA
10. HUNGARY
11. SLOVAKIA
12. CZECH REPUBLIC
13. GERMANY
14. POLAND
15. UKRAINE
16. MOLDOVA
17. ROMANIA
18. BULGARIA
19. TURKEY

20. BELARUS
21. LITHUANIA
22. LATVIA
23. ESTONIA

ICELAND
NORWAY
SWEDEN
FINLAND
DENMARK
NETHERLANDS
BELGIUM
UNITED KINGDOM
IRELAND
LIECHTENSTEIN
LUXEMBOURG
FRANCE
MONACO
RUSSIA
PORTUGAL
ITALY
SAN MARINO
SPAIN
VATICAN CITY
ANDORRA
MALTA
GREECE
CYPRUS

An old and a new boat are on a **fiord** in Norway. A fiord is a long, narrow part of an ocean that flows between mountains.

Europe has many mountains. There are high mountains in Austria, Switzerland, Italy, and Germany. This palace was built on a small mountain in Germany. The name of the palace is Neuschwanstein.

Cities in Europe

More than 820 million people live in Europe, and most of them live in cities. Moscow, London, St. Petersburg, Berlin, Madrid, Rome, and Kiev are the seven largest cities in Europe. There are many more beautiful cities to explore. Visit some of them on these pages.

*Venice stretches across 118 small islands along the Adriatic Sea in northeast Italy. Instead of streets, Venice has **canals**, or waterways. Venice is also known for its wonderful masks and costumes that people wear during Carnival celebrations each year.*

Moscow, Russia's capital city, is in Europe, but most of Russia is in Asia.

Paris is the capital city of France. It is the home of the Eiffel Tower, the tallest building in Paris. Millions of people visit the Eiffel Tower each year.

The beautiful Palace of Westminster, with its clock tower called Big Ben, is in London, England.

Continent of Africa

Africa is the second-largest continent, with more than 50 countries. Some of the countries, such as Madagascar and Seychelles, are islands. The equator passes through Africa. The weather at the equator is hot all year. In fact, most of Africa has hot and sunny weather.

The longest river on Earth, the Nile River, flows through Africa. It runs through the huge deserts of Egypt, as well as through Cairo, Egypt's capital city.

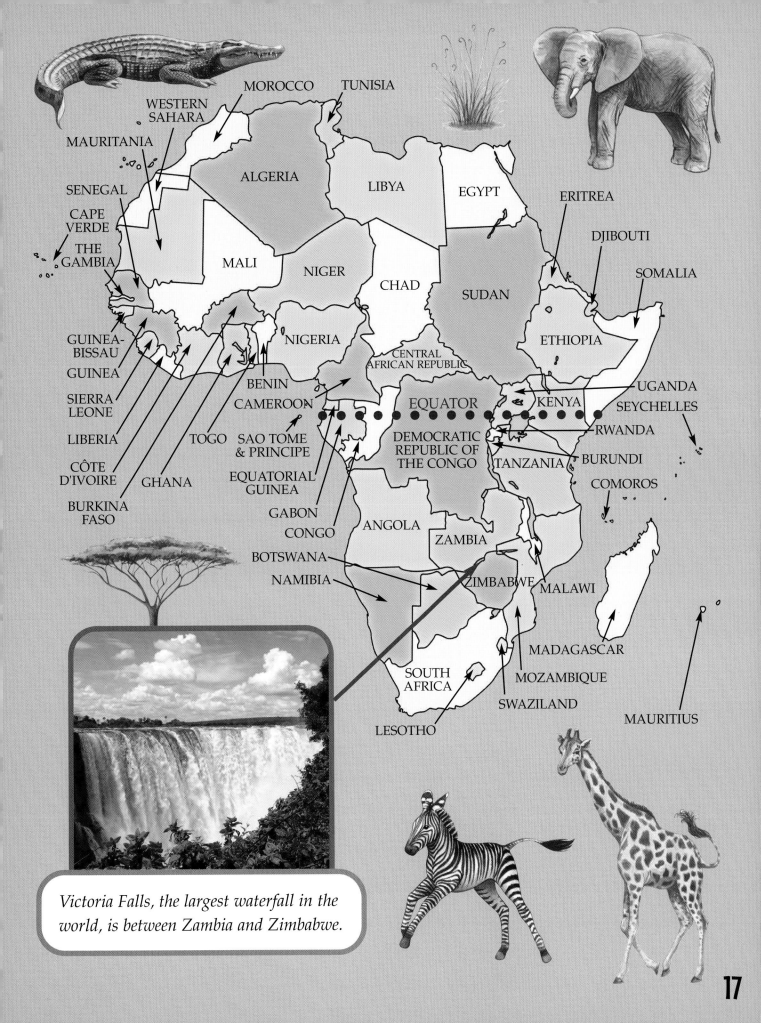

MOROCCO
TUNISIA
WESTERN SAHARA
MAURITANIA
ALGERIA
LIBYA
EGYPT
ERITREA
SENEGAL
CAPE VERDE
DJIBOUTI
THE GAMBIA
MALI
NIGER
CHAD
SUDAN
SOMALIA
GUINEA-BISSAU
NIGERIA
CENTRAL AFRICAN REPUBLIC
ETHIOPIA
GUINEA
SIERRA LEONE
BENIN
UGANDA
SEYCHELLES
LIBERIA
CAMEROON
EQUATOR
KENYA
CÔTE D'IVOIRE
TOGO
SAO TOME & PRINCIPE
DEMOCRATIC REPUBLIC OF THE CONGO
RWANDA
GHANA
BURUNDI
BURKINA FASO
EQUATORIAL GUINEA
TANZANIA
COMOROS
GABON
CONGO
ANGOLA
ZAMBIA
BOTSWANA
ZIMBABWE
MALAWI
NAMIBIA
MADAGASCAR
MOZAMBIQUE
SOUTH AFRICA
SWAZILAND
MAURITIUS
LESOTHO

Victoria Falls, the largest waterfall in the world, is between Zambia and Zimbabwe.

17

Animals in Africa

lion

giraffe

Many kinds of animals live in Africa. They live in different **habitats**. Habitats are the natural homes of plants and animals. **Grasslands** are areas covered in grasses. The grasslands in Africa are called **savannas**. Many animals live on the African savannas. Africa also has mountain, **forest**, and **desert** habitats.

Bushes and trees also grow on savannas. Elephants, giraffes, zebras, lions, and cheetahs are some savanna animals.

baby cheetahs

*Mountain gorillas live in mountain forests. They are **endangered** animals. Endangered animals are in danger of disappearing from Earth.*

scorpion

camel

Desert habitat

There are huge deserts in Africa. Deserts are hot, dry areas. Most animals cannot survive in deserts, but camels, some snakes, and scorpions can. These animals do not need much water.

Saharan horned viper snake

North America

North America is made up of 24 countries. The biggest four are Canada, the United States, Mexico, and Greenland. Some countries, such as the Bahamas and Cuba, are islands. The **climate** of North America is very different from north to south.

The Arctic is the most northern part of North America. The weather there is cold for most of the year.

The middle part of North America has four seasons.

Near the equator, the weather is warm. Florida, Mexico, and the Caribbean Islands have warm weather for most of the year.

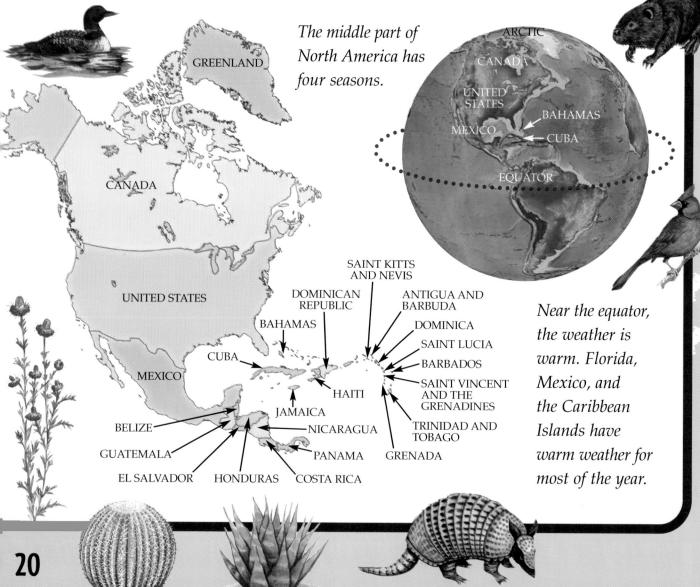

GREENLAND

CANADA

UNITED STATES

MEXICO

CUBA

BAHAMAS

HAITI

JAMAICA

BELIZE

GUATEMALA

EL SALVADOR

HONDURAS

NICARAGUA

COSTA RICA

PANAMA

DOMINICAN REPUBLIC

SAINT KITTS AND NEVIS

ANTIGUA AND BARBUDA

DOMINICA

SAINT LUCIA

BARBADOS

SAINT VINCENT AND THE GRENADINES

TRINIDAD AND TOBAGO

GRENADA

ARCTIC

CANADA

UNITED STATES

MEXICO

BAHAMAS

CUBA

EQUATOR

These polar bears live in the cold Arctic. In North America, the Arctic is in Canada, Greenland, and Alaska. Alaska is part of the United States.

GREENLAND

ARCTIC

ALASKA (U.S.A.)

CANADA

UNITED STATES

MEXICO

It is always warm in the southern parts of North America that are near the equator. These children are swimming in the ocean in Mexico. The child in the middle is dressed for cold weather. What clothes do you wear in winter, spring, summer, and autumn?

Places to see

There are many amazing places to see in North America. Canada, the United States, and Mexico are full of natural and human-made wonders. Niagara Falls, the Caribbean Islands, and the Maya ruins in Mexico are just a few of these.

The Niagara Falls are huge waterfalls on the Niagara River, which separates Canada and the United States. The Falls are wonders of nature!

CANADA

Niagara Falls

UNITED STATES

Maya ruins

MEXICO

CARIBBEAN ISLANDS

Long ago in Mexico, the Maya people built huge cities containing stone palaces, temples, and other buildings. This picture shows part of an old city called Palenque. This city contains beautiful buildings and art.

The Caribbean

The islands of the Caribbean are in the Caribbean Sea. Sunny weather, beautiful beaches, and amazing **coral reefs** make these islands favorite places to visit. A coral reef is an underwater habitat where ocean animals, such as many kinds of fish, sea turtles, and moray eels, live.

sea turtle

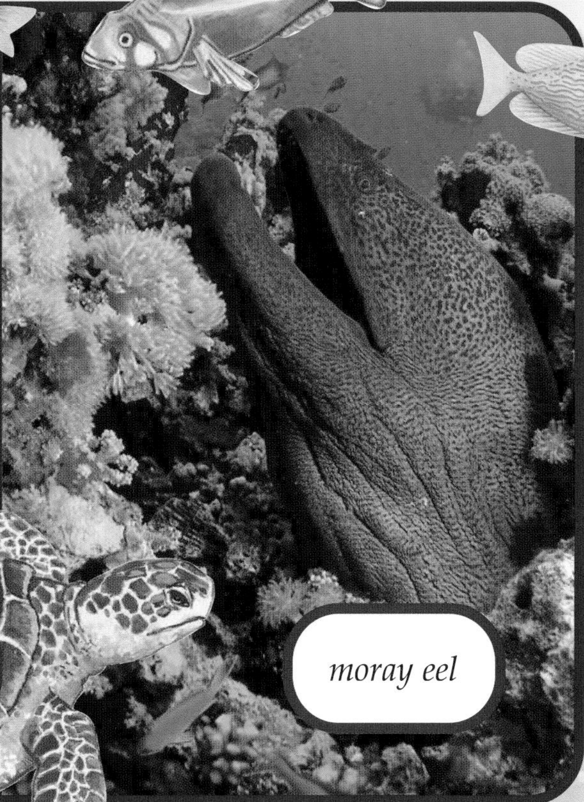

moray eel

23

South America has it all!

South America is a continent between two oceans. On its west coast is the Pacific Ocean. On its east coast is the Atlantic Ocean. The equator passes through the top part of South America. The weather is hot and rainy in the areas close to the equator. The southern part of South America is very cold. Huge **glaciers**, or rivers of ice, can be found here. The picture on the "Contents" page shows a picture of a glacier in Argentina.

A guanaco grazes high up in the Andes Mountains in South America, one of Earth's longest mountain ranges.

GUYANA   SURINAME

VENEZUELA

FRENCH
GUIANA
(part of France)

COLOMBIA

EQUATOR

PERU   BRAZIL

ECUADOR

BOLIVIA

*PACIFIC
OCEAN*

CHILE   PARAGUAY

ARGENTINA   URUGUAY

*ATLANTIC
OCEAN*

FALKLAND ISLANDS
(part of Great Britain)

Twelve countries

The main languages spoken in the twelve countries of
South America are Spanish and Portuguese. The countries
are: Argentina, Bolivia, Brazil, Chile, Colombia, Ecuador,
Guyana, Peru, Paraguay, Suriname, Uruguay, and
Venezuela. Some areas, such as French Guiana and the
Falkland Islands, are not countries. They are **overseas
regions**, or lands, that are part of countries in other
continents, such as France and Great Britain in Europe.

The Amazon

The Amazon rain forest in South America is the biggest **tropical rain forest** in the world. Tropical rain forests grow in areas near the equator, where it is hot and rainy. Most of the Amazon rain forest is in Brazil. The Amazon River, the largest and second-longest river in the world, flows through the rain forest.

leaf frog

Different animals

Many kinds of animals live in the Amazon rain forest. Tree frogs, such as the leaf frog on the right, can be found there. The Amazon River is home to dangerous piranhas and gentle pink river dolphins.

piranha

river dolphin

Golden lion tamarins are small monkeys that live in the trees of the Amazon rain forest.

These are just a few of the other animals that live in the Amazon rain forest.

Brazilian parrot

blue morpho butterfly

Brazilian tapir

southern tamandua (anteater)

anaconda

27

Australia and Oceania

Australia is the smallest continent on Earth. It is completely surrounded by water. Australia is part of a large area called Oceania, which includes thousands of islands. New Zealand, Tahiti, and Fiji are part of Oceania. Many islands in Oceania do not have people living on them.

Water all around

The Pacific Ocean surrounds most of the islands of Oceania, but the Indian Ocean touches Australia's west coast. There are also many seas around Australia, such as the Timor Sea, Coral Sea, Arafura Sea, and Tasman Sea.

TIMOR SEA

ARAFURA SEA

INDIAN OCEAN

CORAL SEA

AUSTRALIA

PACIFIC OCEAN

TASMAN SEA

NEW ZEALAND

Only in Australia

Australia has mountains, forests, grasslands, deserts, and great **rock formations**, or big rocks with unusual shapes. The most famous rock is Uluru, shown below. Australia has thousands of kinds of plants and animals that are not found anywhere else on Earth.

*Koalas and kangaroos are animals called **marsupials**. Most marsupials live in Australia.*

Uluru is also known as Ayers Rock.

Australia and Oceania have beautiful coral reefs, where all kinds of ocean animals live. The Great Barrier Reef is the biggest coral reef on Earth. It is on the east coast of Australia.

AUSTRALIA

Great Barrier Reef

Cold Antarctica

There are no countries on Antarctica, and very few people live there. 48 countries from around the world have signed the Antarctic **Treaty**, or agreement, to protect Antarctica. **Scientists** live on Antarctica to learn more about the land, glaciers, ocean, weather, and animals that live there.

AUSTRALIA

SOUTHERN OCEAN

ANTARCTICA

SOUTHERN OCEAN

SOUTH POLE

SOUTHERN OCEAN

SOUTH AMERICA

AFRICA

The bottom of Earth

Antarctica is in the Southern Hemisphere. The South Pole is in Antarctica. The cold Southern Ocean surrounds this continent. Antarctica is the coldest place on Earth.

Most animals cannot live in Antarctica, but penguins can. Instead of flying, penguins use their wings to swim.

iceberg

pack ice

Ice shapes and forms

Almost all of Antarctica is covered in a thick sheet of ice. In some places, the top of the Southern Ocean freezes into thick sheets of **pack ice** that float in the ocean. **Icebergs** are huge pieces of ice that extend above and below the ocean. The ice formations behind the penguins are icebergs. Sometimes there are large tunnels in the ice, forming **ice caves**.

Glossary

Note: Some boldfaced words are defined where they appear in the book.

archipelago A chain of islands

climate The long-term weather conditions in an area

coral reef An ocean area made up of coral animals

endangered Describing animals that are in danger of dying out

forest An area that has many trees and other plants

habitat The natural place where a plant or animal lives

marsupial A mammal that is born and grows inside its mother's pouch

rock formation A large rock that was shaped by nature

scientist A person who studies or works in science

Index

Learn more about Earth's continents from these other books in the **Explore the Continents** series.